GHOSTS!

M ARTINE B ELLEN

S PUYTEN D UYVIL
New York City

ISBN 978-1-933132-41-9
Ikkyū epigraph translated/version by Stephen Berg from *Crow with No Mouth*. Port Townsend: Copper Canyon Press, 2000.
Cover photograph: Alexey Titarenko, Untitled (Dresses), 1998, Courtesy of Nailya Alexander Gallery, New York, NY
Author photo: Michael Eastman

The author would like to gratefully acknowledge the following journals and anthologies in which some of these poems have appeared:

    "Desire": *The American Poetry Review*
    "DNA": *Famous Reporter* (published in Tasmania)
    "Cubist Winds": *The Colorado Review*
    "Spiritual Mathematics" and "Tribute to H.D.": *Conjunctions*
    "Wool and Water": *First Intensity*
    "Listening in Circles": *In Our Own Words: A Generation Defining Itself*
    "Dearest" and "The Persistence of Passion": *Interim*
    "Any Small Island": *The Literary Review*
    "Connectivity" and "Secretum": *New American Writing*
    "Living with Animals": *26*
    Online chapbook; thedrunkenboat.com: *For the Living*—
        "Fata Morgana" and "For the Living"
    Chapbook; *Malka's Secret Delivery*. G-O-N-G, 2005—
        "Crimes of Living" and "Approximation of Myself"

Much gratitude, also, to Hans Balmes, Barbara Henning, Bradford Morrow, David Rosenboom, Leslie Scalapino Cole Swensen and Tod Thilleman for their invaluable help and inspiration. And gratitude to James Graham.
And in memory of my father.

Library of Congress Cataloging-in-Publication Data

Bellen, Martine.
Ghosts! / Martine Bellen.
p. cm.
ISBN-13: 978-1-933132-41-9
I. Title.

PS3552.E5336G47 2006
811'.54—dc22
2006022046

we live in a cage of light an amazing cage
animals animals without end

—Ikkyū

TABLE OF CONTENTS

GHOSTS!

IN THE COMPUTER

CRIMES OF LIVING

APPROXIMATION OF MYSELF

IN THE MIRROR

TRIBUTE TO H.D.

In Corfu with Freud

I sit in a hotel room, await my father's return. He is with his lover. I, who sit,
Awaiting Freud

Tear jars
       Tense
              Unable to specify the time I mean, the meaning of time

He tells me to stop checking my watch, to trust
My old Janus, guardian of doorways and roads, beloved light-house keeper,
                                    Keeper of the journeying sun

With him I anoint my father's anger, my father's tenderness
Sometimes the twins are sisters

A constellation, circumstance to fit
The garden that corresponds to sky:
Vase of cut stars placed at the temple bough

Like transparencies set before candles in a darkened room
Batlike thought-wings / winds
Confined space of a wicker cage   flickering wicks
Adoring souls, wicked
News of war broke in me   *He said, trust I will not let you break*
He would take me to a world geographically to my dreams
Greece!
Where I saw the writing-on-the-wall   *(Now Gnostic) Know*

                                                                    Thyself

He believed I roamed through dangerous walled cities
Events out of time
What's it like outside   ???   , he asked.   Chalked swastikas down Berggasse
        Fortunes that divine "Hitler Gives Bread"
                To greet the return of the Gods
                                        We roam through dangerous times
Dolls of pre-dynastic Egypt
Thought-winds carry me /   Search-light search
        A dim shape forming on the wall. Foaming swells. Finding
Orange trees in full fruit and flowers outside the window.
        Osage-orange. The walls were ochre.
The house in early shadow. Light on shadow not the other way around. Object projected
        From my brain, basin, buried mind
        Washstand/saucepan or tripod
        Of prophecy. Our thoughts translated into
        Secreted language. Entombed.

Monument wall / will

Between ink, space flies, flanked by butterfly and dying

          Psyche

Death: You can't always get more than your due.
Apollo: We weep when the goods are destroyed.

And how do we know when He has died   ???   When we walk down Wall Street and see no
Centaurs—Centaurs who once felt everything ...

[The following scene takes place in a room on the other side of the wall.]

This is said by me and a voice I'm overhearing that would say what I'd say, if I were in the next room on the other side of the wall:

> I am disturbed he has no idea death won't kill him
> He will shed his locust-husk
> The sun-conscious world of sleep
> That final healing when he sloughs off his skin.

*

If a woman plants herself by a river,
Gods of trees, air, water
Grace her as a poplar, mulberry, laurel.

Globes of gold
Apples, flecked with russet
A skeleton leaf

Her daughter bears the weight of the lost
Child—never grows beyond eight pounds,
Even after she's agéd, wizened—Mother
Carries her in the fifth pocket.—Mother is a poem.

Outline in shadow, a lone symptom or inspiration.

Sappho

Shaft of scarlet lilies, crushed hyacinth, sea-grass gold,
Leaf melody of unfinished rhymes, of rocky rhythms, rocks
Polished by water
                    Water beating ragged edges; they are never finished,
Flowers blow through flowing water, not a streaming song
But water's wayfaring spirit, its crystal myrtle-berry.

The daughter of God
Chariot pulled by sparrows aquiver across high, steep air
And none alive remembers you, gray among ghosts

Niké, the winded runner, the wingless runner, the girlish black-eyed girl.

Desire has shaken her skeleton
Leaf of the osage-orange flutters in charmed air
From inside out she shakes to escape
The ache of dancing flame pillages her walls of flesh and downy hair.

Chats to Cats

The Old Man of the Sea, Sigmund Freud, stood before me,
He stands before me now seventy-two years later,
A little lion-like creature shuffles in my direction.
Everyone carries an animal in them.

War is not over.

Our deep place where we hate—where Thoth and Apollo reside
Riding a gap-toothed goat.

Last night Freud heard the familiar siren-shrieks, then the soul-shattering "all clear."

Danger is out there—the Professor's eternal preoccupation, occupation.

Nemean lion clearing birds from the mind's rafters, fate.

Planting his steadfast foot in the stream of consciousness
Each line in a poem can't avoid acting as a series of questions
That stands half-hidden in the river reeds watching over
A life that's being born. This is life—see!

His is a frail bridge, strong enough for the Gods, who weigh little.
His is a bridge only few can cross. The building construction
Of phantasms across the bridge are lines of poetry. We reach deep

Inside ourselves and become Gods, light enough to pass, to cross
The rickety bridge over to a housing project
Made of poems. —Mid-income.

He is comfortable leaving this set of phenomena

Guardian of all beginnings

DESIRE

Gathered flames, each wingflap folding
An alternative to the body

        See her offer up variants of self (flying things)
        (crawlers) (things that swim)
—Damselfly, Schwinn, midge, buoys—
Our eyes shut restore to ash (sublimated)

Cinderella wanted to fuck & fuck,
     Bop, don
        Fairy threads. Two strangers
     In psyche's sphere
Will never know themselves. Reconstruction of their
Knowledge (not about but in)
Forms one half of irrational.

A waster vaster world
As body emerges, emigrates through day.

     Lost
     Power to unassuming form,
        Pool
     Of hair, eye, liquid, idea—

How she braided echoing heart bells,
        Cleaned, dusted, mopped herself
    Magnificent frigatebird
    Screaming mind to overplow

"Before supper she's Kantian, after dessert Nietzschean"

        Still a little interior
        The doctor strokes his penis absently
        Arrives to remain
        Is a rested
            Strength
                Wearied by frequent remembrance
        Arrives at the stop

                "Freudian?"

Cattails, details, denials

        His hand—a pack of wild cards—
        Between her legs curiosities—
        He opens sesame, she robs
        His control, aviator, magicians sing

Sound felled deep
A wishing well

She: vascular seams, stitch marks; stretchmarks

Spring from her / attenuate silence

He puts his soil on one thigh.

Becomes hillsides.

Handbreadth

Plotline wanders over.

Someplace it has never been.

When a Yogavatar flies toward birth
Using sonar & sonata
Reseeding hermetic secrets

Palace of pleasure
Pattern of shame

Butterfly bush

Wind—(describe its
Location   history)

[day,
　　　decay,
　　　　　evening,
　　　　　　　primrose]

Upon looking at a nymph?
　　　　Eating an apple?
What during midwinter twilights

LISTENING IN CIRCLES

The lore of friendship, lure of love,
Or that devil Musboot, Lord of Lies

Scatterings of a soul.

If revolutions of his character collide
With an alien force, and they collude
In the opposite of truth, he becomes foolish,
And though his soul appears to destroy
It itself is conquered.

Each body has one shadow
Each self any number of shadowy images.
Which are your counterfeit countenances?

Particles of him
Remote from his shape.

When she denies the shadowy lives he's leading,
The lies he's leading her to believe,
When he whispers, *Don't look back* …

"As being is to becoming, so truth is to belief."

Haunted house memory—innominate.
      Upstairs, Golem hangs in soiled corners,
Outside
      Singes her interior—sings.

            Only the closest cell can destroy those closest to it
            How a molecule
            Transforms its state of being by the processes it endures
            The way fish control seas

      The way a woman sometimes holes up in her closet
      Her clothes—panties, powders, powers pulverized.

Vulva: vulnerable: vound: voman: I vant to be
                  A revolving film fast-forwarded
      Not rewinding, resolving in love unreturned & life unlived.

Disgrace: the deprivation of beauty, grace,
A salve that hides the immediate wound without healing:
Humiliation.

A friend in the shadow, a fiend
    The curio dealer at the carney
    Her house of ghost daggers
    The audience applauds, appalled—weeps, woo-woos
        In a sequin bikini she curtsies
        It's a trick!
        She's dead.

He devotes himself to the loveliness
Of form,
Absences of one sort or another.

It seems to her, since deception exists
Likenesses can appear anywhere, everywhere,
Cloaked in subtle chicanery
The art of creating semblance
Shadow or lie woven into reflection's intensity,
Speculum of simulacra.

SPIRITUAL MATHEMATICS

Ecstasy in the buried garden.
                    Unconscious
Dominion. Birdcrumbs
        Follow flight backward on the screen
Against all odds, to some original time.

            Unrecognizable now that he's
                              The stuff of cloud—
        As though space could rest. Sound
                        Connecting lies to truth.

If negative integers (-1, -2) constitute pre-quantities—
in this instance pre-birth—; and if positive integers
constitute present quantities, such as a tiger flying
through air; then what manner of integer would describe
this tiger whose flight [escape] ceases while
his force springs forth? The tiger is no longer pre nor qua,
but remains matter, neither created nor destroyed.
What ghost sum accompanies his breakaway?

A conjunction of two ideas, impossible to unite without her
So delicate,
Imperceptible but here
Remains.

With eyes open she echoes that dream. Fabricates a world,
Forgets, or awakens
On to alternate scenes
Hides in her mother's voice,
Offbeat talents, mascara,
The seditious garden.

In the empire of stars
A sun determines
A body's course.
She extinguishes a candle, burns incense,
Suns of many colors shine.
Now aqua, now lavender,
Divergent waves reflect back
A solar system of give and take.

Another view. Imagine: negative integers constitute pre-birth;
       0—that nothing-but-space-and-balance
              Circa (?) living;
                     And positive integers,
                                 postlife,
            The infinity we're ! to face   :(

Whose likeness from vacuumed mass is loosed on the world?
       Whose feline eyes?
Here are photographs with webbed illumination,
    Pixilated showers,
              Raw exposures, too contrasted to reckon
    Like staring through a star.

She asks over silence,
         Evades contact through stillness, remoteness
                 That threatens a flier, obscures
    A species of spirit that leaps into fog,
         Commits suicide of sense.

If she inverts the graph on which her point is plotted

She will vanish

Unable to see the circle's center

To know herselves:

The moon's migraine

Uproarious pregnancy.

O tiger beyond physics.

FOR THE LIVING—GEISTPHILE

If body is an impermanent manifestation of infinite spirit
Can anyone deny space is haunted?

If love is an expression that death
Seduces   hardens

      Ghost lover,

      You have been gone
      For some time now.
      At first I didn't notice.
      Like a ghost, love slipped out, like sex, your ghost limb

      You say you love me, I feel you
      In abstentia.
      "To ghost" means take passage on a ship. Without
      Meaning the world is hollow.

Parallel word in which he is husband / servant / enemy / father—
Why therapy exists
And one cannot be separate from another
Without disturbing a complex
Entanglement.

To pray is to break silence, break bread.
To pray is to partake
In the dead.

What's not fluid?
The mind, wind, wants
Stability, to understand
Has no coordinates.

Quantum entanglement, their fates inextricably linked.
Multiple answers detained through superposition or multiverse.
She had the chance to love a man but chose a ghost.
He will make me happy, she told her friends. He touches a part of me that's dead.
More of her became dead the longer they loved.

As a haunted human she moved away from certainty,
Moved toward what she wanted
To be certain. Ha! Ha!

The probability of finding a lover at a point in space.

She found the lover exists as possibility, therefore always exists—
Lost
Potential.

A web of relationships and interrelationships
Bound by boundaries of body.

If the space we inhabit is shared by all spirit
Unlimited realm
                    Circuit
                                Frequency
Unrelenting.

Our bodies, containers we pour out
Slowly until we're left
To choose the extent of ourselves.
Distance that separates one event from another. Soul.
Like the sun eight minutes in the past. How close is that in space?
Solar. Look at Saturn! Has it passed your past? Or Pluto?
More moons. More. More.

Fear she's not loved, therefore value neutral
As though love were the sun. Blinding.
Must not look directly. Like God / Truth

When / where space-time curves nothing can escape it.
It captures me and I become it, therefore cannot see it.
No communication signal breaks free
                    Can you *know* loneliness?

DNA

A national survey reports one quarter of adults
                              Experience off-the-Richter-scale loneliness
                    (Easy peasy)
As the lonely-sensitive brain archives threats,
                              Social relationships or intimate betrayals,
          Compared to nonlonelies who seek relational integration.

Our architects of loneliness blueprint structures and underlying proteins,
                    Which translate, "I knew it was coming"
                              as a + or - verdict
                                        (Prisoner's dilemma)

          Hostage #3 pacifies her social pain.
                    Survival depends on collective ability.

Her behavior controlled by tweeters or a high-frequency console,
          The fatal production that induces belief in mirages
          And heightened microawakenings.

                    Organized tourist buses with cybernetic prostheses
          Cross state lines to "New Life"
                    Dead-ended by the cul de sac "Need."

The group of lonelies tours a Tastee Snack factory, psycho-physically
                              Exhausted, propensity toward ecstasy, pilgrimage
              For heroic existence. But these *petit mort* yield no resolution
         And day-trippers not comfortable with sunyata
Continue suffocation.
                        Sentiment constructs archaeological layers of consciousness,
                        Sentient Creatures.
                        Sedimentary particles of telematic energy
                                        Or invisible tele-beings (ghost friends)
                        As temporary artificial surface
         Imperative for the future of loneliness and its social intention.

Secretum

So, little Book, I bid you flee the haunts of men and be content to stay with me, true to the title I have given you, "My Secret": and when I would think upon deep matters, all that you keep in remembrance that was spoken in secret, you in secret will tell to me over again."   —Francesco Petrarca

S. Augustine: Who goes there and of what do you dream?

He recognized the gravity of the disease,
                                    Which is life,

And most give themselves prematurely.

So why don't we detach from our bodies?
Occupy mind?
        Little birds, they say, take so much delight in their own singing that they can sing
Themselves to death.
                        Makes you forget your weakness for God,
                                How when he swore he'd be faithful
Self-reliance vanished with language—Inadequate for ideas and passion,
Makes you
Grossly underestimate Eros and Thanatos antimatter

Or despair—the utterly insane evil of the body,
And most men give.

        Gatekeeper: Who goes there? (trans., Who are you?)

The word as flesh the word is God through whom the world is passed
With no extension in space, with or without limit.

Petrarca: Death in the locked treasure chamber as an offering
            To accept distance from understanding.

S. Augustine: Have we rested long enough? Are we awake enough?
                                  (For absolute extinction)

      NoFace: I am the ghost of the father.

Petrarca: However diligently we seek, we never obtain our aspiration.
          God, unchanged, makes all things new,
          Transforms our desires till they appear before us unrecognizable.

Bellen: He awoke in me and saw the infinite, concealed in code
    oxoxoxoxoxoxooxoxoxoxoxoxoxoxoxoxoxoxoxoxoxoxoxoxox

The scroll he eats, internalized secrets.
How hideous his body becomes
Charged with the course of stars, properties of herb, stone.

To desire ardently then to sleep
        He turns himself into wind. That is procreation:

Inventing an abstract form of self-discovery—Internal intangible.
From the outside:
        Death. The loved one lives in the tenement memory,
     On the Lower East Side. Where immigrates congregate,
        Dominating the past and indeed isolation becomes the country.

The existence of nonexistence,
        The resistance to yield up secrets recorded in memory
          Or musical notation,
     Informed by divine intension. Memory as place or activity. Converted
        Memory-shards of past us(es) our past uses us into
                  Becoming a coherent other.
                   Orderly narration
Of self. What part of the mountain am I?

S. Augustine, Petrarca, NoFace, Bellen: The constitution of a self
                        Is its surrender.

S. Augustine: Have you so entirely forgotten your miseries? Don't you remember
that you are mortal? Miseriarum ne tuarum sic prorsus oblitus es? An non te
mortalem esse meministi?

Memory as sickness
Of imagination. Concupiscence.

IN THE COMPUTER

When her pictorial world dissolves into color
                    Replicating nature from within
                                    Its breathing
                                        Space.
For instance, not perceiving the persistence of light in her life
                                        Despite intermittent beams / Not *that*
                                        Which is impossible to perceive / hides

In "Time"
            Programmed into the brain, it moves her
            From one scene to the next. The way she arrives anyplace is a mystery

Her ride, relatively flicker free.

But stills sometimes linger, still
                        Sometimes
                                She can't believe she's moving. A stalled planet.

& If she suffers insight into her limited perspective, then what?
If she glimpses dark periods of nothingness that compose half the frames she inhabits?

Invisible sites define her narrative /

*

In the booth, vortex of powers turned on.

Keep 'em in the dark

He shouts over scraps of evidence while his female projection talks

Of a near fatal accident,

As though that's not our entire lives.

The detour he takes through the matter of women,

Upmappable terrain / cut, bleed

She touches his / _art

The blind spot

Buried between arm and wing

Seeing motion

As psychological illusion. What can be felt /

[Believed]

When her cell dissolves

Not in the past but a parallel present

More than one Martine simulcast

Scared & sacred negative misprison.

Shadowman sculls a silhouetted ferry,

memento mori, hauling fishes or silver strand,

    River of stars; sky of leaping fish,

            When Myo received that luminous night,
            "Cleansed of sores go home without your body—
            Someone will present you to yourself."

      Her current switches
             Calming, common
She steps into a lemon eclipse—erotic blue

& Resigns moon viewing to late autumn
            As senses fell a winter tree & light
    In a backyard falls unobstructed, lets
Like blood from a vein.

Clay of waves, waveforms, essential tensions seeking equilibrium

Dream wounds with vast structures of inner life, in her life
Or brain limits speed of emotion-thought, assigns meaning.
The chemical reaction responsible for significance
Or order of events critical to the development of self-image.

In a city of edifice, buildings reign
Musical space-time

Confluence of forces
Intangible

      Parting wings, panting winds, braving deeps

Or electromagnetic force divines the ocean floor toward her,
What she feels when walking east and west. A map made of inflection,

Implication

Still, before this moment *this* moment
Hadn't existed. Time as an organizational device—such as a filing cabinet.
No repeating *This*. Proxy.
Approximation [of who I was] (She). The ersatz attempts to stay
Awake, will continue to be her [the old me, the newer one to come]
                Though by another animator
                        Imitator.
                  Wander-souls seek suicide.

Who sees the change in gods? I mean guards.

With the notion of time erased, it has been tough for dreamers, of late.
                    Not just eternity but infinity.

"Well, I'll eat it," said Alice/Myo, "and if it makes me grow larger, I will reach the key; and if it makes me grow stronger, I'll creep under the door; so either way I'll get into the garden, which is *all* I care about!"

Our investigation is grammatical, sheds light on our problem by clearing away misunderstandings between forms of expression in different regions of language.

To be dying is to be living, to be living is to be dying.

If the Hara is empty spirit as we wander through form. Sound mountain. Wind engenders time. Breath: wind. Nonwind, nonbreath engenders timelessness. Nonlessness. For those who have re-leased breath, housed in it, firing down freeways. Relinquish. Clinking bell.

This Matter beyond correspondence

So, for instance, love is syntactical in nature, protected by sexual organ.

Certain aspirations nontransferable.

The similarities between the sentences "I'll keep it in mind" and "I'll keep it in this box" can lead one to think of the mind as a thing like a box with contents of its own.

The doctor instructed, "You must not give her any more till your lips are quite rested." "But, you see, I owe her a hundred and eighty-two."
Tears ran down the doctor's cheeks, and he offered, "Send your kisses in a box."

The muscles of your mind will tire out if you believe such impossible things and you'll grow so weak you won't be able to believe the simplest true things.

One hundred eighty-two kisses arrived Special Delivery, I believe.

Inventers of mirrors and minor notes. Venters of anger. Venders of illusion.
The illusion that time is an excuse to forget only *This* instant exists.

Though she has identity plates to drive through a lucid state, the order of critical events
Altered and she has became other

That things might change or cease, that they might not

And so it was: she, now, only ten-inches high, and her face brightened at the thought that
she was the right size for going through the little door into that lovely garden.

In the garden of melody, listen to shiny stones, harp sparrow, and the wavering road. Weeds
overtake plot. She roots them out, the din, colors, cloud evanescent.

If nothing is true than anything is possible.
   We are creatures in minds
    Of others: musk, lichen,
      Bits of landscape, stamen
   Assorted forms simultaneously

To remember love has no one
    Meaning

Desire opiating the present. Before she knows it
A variety of bodies have been lived in
[Nightshade, touch-me-not],
One minded like the weather, most unquietly.
Collected miracle, collective miracle.

Myo said speech defines water levels. Saliva, pond, proud body;
Aquavit ocean and disrobing it. Robbing its moods, moaning waves, deepening
Roots,
      Intensely intellectual and erotic, expands form, mind ground.
                        How a fluid transports her surrender, beneath her

Lips and tongue stir mindlessly
Breath cruises the unexplored
When someone enters your life and jolts you into fluency.

She was sent an attachment, only 30KB; couldn't open the file or
Leave [love, believe] herself.

     (he, the attachment she tried to detach from, contained movement
                       Of a present
        Dreamroom, abound WorldWideWeb.com
     Not minding no-mind or that knot
        Apart from her,
           Not part of her)

Self-secrets uncovered in mediary diaries where memory is shed as being-time
Stretches beyond birth without concept spreads limitlessly.

A soul-stone the size of Polaris
Stored in a mason jar crammed with lost buttons from bygone eras
Or stuffed with nuts and bolts, greasy
Closures.

Miles of her. Separate.

Indigenous deities, mountain sprites.

Myo lives TiVo
                    Computer headspace, digitalized storage,

How she organizes herself/time internally. Mental tempora.
                                        In- and outside travel
Varying speeds, multitudinous directions.

Ouch!

Monk A: What have you done in a lifetime?

Monk B: Eaten a little midday and slept a few hours at night.

Monk A: Tilled the land, harvested its cornucopia.

> *Sun falls through the belly of mountain. Moon crescent*
> *Pocks earth with shadow. Oceans wave &*
> *Boulder. Nothing*
>> *Special.*

The wizard comments: One is judged not by how deeply one loves

but by how deeply one is loved—[couldn't be further from the truth]

> *We seek it far away, what a pity!*

Invisible thread or Borg-like interdependence

> While wreckless gods build firewalls
>> We Delicious pick, encrypt, decode, cut loose

The metaphysics of self-conception

> Paves a perpetual identity destiny (the etiology
>> Between attachment to self and independence
>>> {In-dependence
>>> Deep time comprehended

In a trance

> Vanished.

Like Osiris who was gathered from land- to bodyscape
I re-member my father by my heart
Sow him from pieces of me, (farther from my truth)
The wondrous phenomenal mansion of who I became
Without thinking.

The vase body

Flickering of a lantern like the light of firefly, friendly fire, like prana roused
Out of Code Blue.
My self-vision bleeding to emptiness,
Wires, pipes, tubing or
Puffins loosed with red ribbons dangling off wings,
Beautiful but still
Strings, so attached to freedom, to sky.
Mind capturing
Mirror of insight walking through the town of appearances,
Apparitions of intelligence, edifice, elevator.

Based on hearing
The awareness-holders
Protected over lifetimes
By the heart practice.
Secret Master Hero Stainless Steel—Subway, steal me away,
After which I'm dissolved. As a result, realizations spontaneously spring. Vital wind blows
evenly. I forget about the appearance of life. My father was heroic,
nonmaterial, nonactual.
My code breaker. Not making it known, even to the Wind-Ear transmission. We gather with
inner offerings. Offing.
Impermanency rings with the concept of notions. Suture-needles & needs & pins
Undermines metaphysics of the individual (underpinnings), rendered empty of essence
because of the proximity of death—who I am without you.

IN THE MIRROR

LIVING WITH ANIMALS

Her room lit by the cache of a thousand creatures
                                        Their thorny hooded habits

                        With shrew-nets, dream-rods,
She catches her keep.

                                        *

                Nocturnal spirits play secretive, rarely seen, most at home
                                        On ground but climb trees
Or hyphenate wing and air — soaring through the transparent prison,
                Partaking in oral transportation,
                Moving through sound and speech.

                                        *

None lightened without adding light
                    Flavor for euphony
Like cheesecake batter in a yellowware bowl
                    Craft the body spiritual and it will glow,
            A moon spoon for mixing words,
How co-life aspires.
Headlamps hold night-frogs. Dixie Cups, polliwogs.

                              *

Falling from the sky and floating, a melody
        Leaves
                Its unfinished line
                In memory

            The soul's sphericity. Through marbleized
                Eyes. Tambourines.
                    Cat's harlequin carnival.

                              *

A round-up of abstracted Arabians

                              Hazy paint drays

                Quicken / drear

Variation of song and sense.

                         In one fugue state or another

This fairy ring of yearlings trailing an areola along nerves

                              Of insect's iridescent wing.

                                   *

           Aristophanes, Hitchcock

                 Draw light on imaginings

                         Hawk & owl descend during new moon

           Unlike cumulus cloud pets, the dispossessed

X ray through darkness,

                 Break an oath that binds bird to bird.

           A constellation of warblers undulate in sealed captivity

By her bedside

                 Rests a jar of black glass

                         She breathes the breath of flight,

Cardinal points.

*

Once upon a time, they shed
        Their scales,
               Tumbling into reverie.
Pressure on night's reduced darkness
           Or failure to adhere
To demands of the waking dead: Their double, amphibious lives
        Perpetually encircling a soul describing escape:
                         The haunt.

CONNECTIVITY

A flickering of spirit runs and reruns
Traversing sky, our domed cineplex,
Emotional power, electric too

Such radiance and obfuscation move us
    To marvel at a skeleton tree,

        A cottonwood, parched roots delve into earth,
        Knows intimately her
                Dark spaces

And delicate shades of expression.

Mediated tree and immediate tree
    The essence of tree
        Limned with rusty dusk and cobalt ice,

A generic tree and the pin oak you plant,
    The concentrate tree of deferred orgasm
        Sets branch aflame with apricot finch.

The sweet tree bejeweled in sky-blue berries.

    Wind or no wind,
    A closed world guarded by luster

For spectator and specter alike

Vision of tree as pillar
Of luminosity,

A pound of tempest weighs the same as still pond water

Not a fiction of fixed time but fluctuating contents
Not the ridged tree,
Nor the tree that bridges
Mineral to high-riding clouds of dawn,

No matter how
Far back in memory you travel, the tree is there.

When you lost
Your way, miles separated God from nature
(God—the goal, nature—its process).

Truly, morning would not pass
Were it up to the former.

CUBIST WINDS

To discover a tree in his ear,
Birds in that tree.
A clearing, charmed stream
Coils the breeze.

       Sibilance
       Sibilance

Everything's motile
Composed of iron (for might),
             Sulfur (change),
                    Water (flexibility)
Add dust and dearth.

       *

When hurricane emanates a void
                    The impermanence of beauty

      Doors swing inward
                 An opening onto himself.

                  *

If one walks through a front
      Visibility gloom;
            Instilled with the immeasurable dimensions
Of spirit, though blind to his nature—a weatherscape in proportion
          To what she trusts is
                 Not pure emptiness.

The way an easterly
        Penetrates him
Cave-swallows
        Excavate,
Tunnel through his know-how or nest
In naturally occurring holes. How he struggles to receive deities
           Sacred bondage

        Whisper song
          Between wind & weather

An intellectual   *mistral*
Passionate   *sirocco*

Frightened   *willy willy*
                  Lightning
                      Up its elephantine trunk
                      Out through branches and leaves
                      If roots are damaged, its line dies

         Cloud lore
         Passerine

With an eyedropper
Kidnapping delicate dreams
Progeny of intimacy.

Identifying the course his mind rages,
Its incline and turbulence.
                    The *haboob* spiraling sand thousands of feet above.
                                Specks disseminating
                                                Light-years westward.
                                Dust chokes memory
                        Clogs the heart.

How to find land when winds have left atmosphere structurally damaged

                    The loss of his glow system. Pool
    Filled with sunbeams.   Currents float hollow stalk and bone.

            Even a container (exists/doesn't) for winds
                    Ocean basin, brain,
                            Crusty earth storing magma,
        Luminous little begging bowl of vibrant determination.

                                *

If small clouds of late noon melt on dusk,
        The gentleness of dawn
                                Dew, frost,
                Fog evaporate
        As though they never were.

                        That which appears
As opposed to what is. Optics or perspective.

                Answers run out
                        Like breath
                                How a cone connects cloud with
        Surface
                        Of water-whirling air
An inland phenomena that occurs when radiance first
                                Reflects on his face.

FATA MORGANA

1.

She removes herself from the rational realm of feelings

      Flooded by a prevailing intelligence

Where she hides for longer than a mood.

That which is "in the air,"
A surround environment, not all of her own making.
She constructs its interpretation and moves inward. Sound

                                            Outside boundaries.
For instance, architectural surrounds built with language-doors, walls,
Floors from words. Would she open the window? double paned,
Unusually weighty. A vowel she looks through to see changes
In weather, to see outside the confines of her scape.

When the surround she understood encountered the surround that was.
Plate disturbance traumatizes earth. Bends her, morphs her
                                    Bedrock.

2.
Two-thirds of life she's unconscious,
                   A romp through the privacy of land not created.
Splinter souls—sinuosities or organic forms flattened to fill shadow space,

The body's music:

Awakens for her dream, sleeps off continuity.

But for the sake of survival she believes what appears to be
A one-point perspective system
In which recessional lines join where they vanish.
Creating distortions, objects skew.

When the assumption of a system is altered, the space it describes
Changes in unforeseen ways.

Horizontals and verticals support the couple's stability, and belief in realism
Fades.

To scale a domestic scene
She sees her point dematerialize while what surrounds her
Increases size, clarity of focus.

Within her flat canvas exists immeasurable depth,
Uncountable colors, interminable death.
To satisfy her need for proof,

If she believes nothing,
Vacant imagination acts as symptom.

3.

Since the surround exists only in the present
Impressions made on space erase. Language-doors,
-walls, -ceilings repainted and papered, no pentimento,

The Vermeer-like canvas tips to spill pigment till she drips
Into a de Kooning disaster, crystalline blue melds into muddy brown,
Finely crafted cabinets into the notion of a knee. Her disfigured
Physiognomy flattened as foreground in the surround,
                                        Chimera of a narrative sphere.

ANY SMALL ISLAND

Under a canopy of fetid fruit, we drank Wu Wei:
Fun getting dizzy, stalked by sun circles,
A battalion of Radio Flyers, getaways
To paper scenery—trump l'oeil and abandoned dolls—family stand-ins.

How to lasso tots that stray?
Horsehair spilling from a pillow!
A moment's thought is passion's passing bell (Keats).

Twine, fish-line fused into balls of birdcrumbs. Attempting escape. Ha!
Sight of the peppermint residence seduced Hansel and Gretel.
Who could resist a fudge roof? Truffle oleanders?
Wildly infinite hope, worth a death. Scampering away on all fours.
And Granny promising prajna.
She thatches a fagot fresh for witching hour. Her too-long schnozzle.

Mouth full of burnished gold from peanut-butter-dipped LSD
Phewy!

*

Off the clipper, Mannahatta buried in trees, smells of tar,
Salt. Why hadn't I reloaded my bazooka?
Memory of gallows: the woman hanged, a grand spirit. Hellcat Bubby
Trained me to boil charms—melding tongue, spells,
Spicey melody, pirouetting on the scrubbed linoleum.
My heart misplaced for years in my knee,
Stitched at St. Vincent's by the resident figure-flinger.

   Pigeon leaps through air—exotic dancer—
Floats above the floor of light, and she feels Gran in her ghost heart,
(I am she). How many souls haunt this cadaver? Downtown streets circle
In indecision. Her trust built by finding avenues back to midtown.
And there, among the fields of corn and chrome, she hides,
Sponges color from her surroundings,
No active participation or resistance
Sleep lingers all our lifetime about our eyes (Emerson).
Any stability, even solitary confinement, is preferable to change.
She knows where she thinks she is. But when is she?
Watchmen swinging bells and lanterns.

*

Powerless to control phenomena at a distance
Therefore unable to judge veracity. The way her past reveals
Itself when she can no longer effect it. Only one hundred wanderers
(Aborigines, colonists) remain after the massacre. She meanders
Through the Brambles, cadences of connections
Cut. Screech owl. Running shad. Fossiled schist.
To construct form out of the history of her private landscape:
At last locked up, her body growing out of bounds.
Wooden clothespins affixing her bloomers
Across a field of red poppies. *That life is a suck and a sell, and nothing*
Remains at the end but threadbare crepe and tears (Whitman).

Doesn't touch ground, but arabesques
Darkness. She knows good dragons inject
Bad girls with goop and wing. Spiritual kingdom
Of gooseberry pie.

Look! She's a paper doll
Yearning to shed toddler togs attached at shoulder and hip by folded tabs.
Convert the realm,
Unreal, into fashion—Dolce & Gabbana mules,
Clingy Chloé frock! Shocked back into the blind-glass, not looking,
Exquisitely, painfully harmless.

A compulsion race runs ahead of the coming storm. Her skin and bones
No longer the sliding door to lock out sound
Thinking. Missing girl beside her doppelganger.
Today she feels violet: this workbook of problems open on her lap.

After so much growing, it stops, forever
Everlasting faster than time can weather.

Dearest,

In the summer of 365, when the sea withdrew in Cyprus
And stone was spewed from the living earth, young parents
Cradled their offspring in burning flesh and tenderness.
The father, arching like a pediment, sheltered his wife
From entombing mortar. His arms shielding her
Breasts. The supple flesh of their four hands
Protecting baby's skull and spine. Snapped neck, wing
Bone clipped. How heroic and fragile
They are, stilled for eternity before dawn.

This morning, the sun streaks magenta and tangerine.
A deep calm stifles the earth.
When you withdrew, stone and fire were hurled into the heavens,
Torn asunder. So fragile are tendon, synapse, which plait
And protect love. The hard parts that fossilize, soft parts
Vaporize, like shadow-remnants of a nuclear storm. Buried
Memories quake. My love, what is left
This daybreak as we rise in the quiet and safety of our shelters?

As ever,

Finding my way back from the underworld.

MARTINE BELLEN is the author of six collections of poetry including the *Vulnerability of Order* (Copper Canyon Press); *Tales Of Murasaki and Other Poems* (Sun & Moon Press), which won the National Poetry Series Award; and *Places People Dare Not Enter* (Potes & Poets Press). Her libretti include *Ovidiana*, an opera based on Ovid's *Metamorphoses* (composer, Matthew Greenbaum) and *AH!* opera no-opera, in collaboration with composer David Rosenboom, (for more information, visit www.ah-opera.org), which made its world premiere at REDCAT in L.A. Her novella, $2X^2$, is published by BlazeVOX [books]. She has been a recipient of a residency at the Rockefeller Foundation Center in Bellagio, a New York Foundation for the Arts Fellowship, a Fund for Poetry grant, and the American Academy of Poets Award. Bellen is a contributing editor of the literary journal *Conjunctions* and is on the Belladonna* Collaborative.

S P U Y T E N   D U Y V I L
Meeting Eyes Bindery
Triton